Nature Near and Far

HOUGHTON MIFFLIN HARCOURT
School Publishers

Contents

Phonics

Words with <u>th</u> Read each word. Tell which words have <u>th</u>. Use two <u>th</u> words in a sentence.

tick	hat	bat	thud
thick	that	bath	math
hen	tin	pat	this
then	thin	path	with

Seth and Beth

by Anna Guzman
illustrated by Piero Corva

Seth and Beth met at the path.
Beth has a big map. It can help.
They will go and see Bob Frog.

This trip is far.
Seth and Beth pass Ben. Ben
can see them. Seth tips his cap.
Then Ben tips his cap.

This trip is far.

Beth and Seth pass Sam. Sam
can see them. Seth and Sam tip
their hats.

Beth and Seth pass Huck Duck.
They are at Blue Pond. Huck
can see them.

"Where is Bob Frog?" Beth yells.

"Does Bob Frog live here?"
Seth asks.
"Bob Frog is in this pond,"
Huck quacks.

"Get up, Bob Frog!" Seth and
Beth call. "Play with us! This is
fun! It is fun."

Book Information

Book Parts Remember that the **author** writes a story. The **illustrator** draws the pictures. The **title** is the name of the story.

What is the title of this story? Who is the author? Who drew the pictures?

Phonics

Words with <u>th</u> Read each sentence. Tell which picture goes with the sentence. Then point to and read the <u>th</u> words.

1. Jack has a thick pad.

2. Beth has a thin pen.

3. Rip gets a bath.

Zeb Yak

by Jane Tyler
illustrated by Katherine Lucas

This is Zeb. Zeb is a yak. Zeb is
a little yak. Zeb is not big yet.

Zeb will get big and look like this.
Zeb will be like his big dad. Then
Zeb will go thud, thud, thud.

Zeb is with his mom. His mom will
eat grass. Zeb can eat grass.
Then Zeb and Mom will nap.

Zeb and his mom and dad live
on this cold hill. Lots of yaks live
with Zeb and his mom and dad.
Yaks cut big paths on the hill.

Big yaks go thump, thump, thump.
Big yaks go thud, thud, thud.
The paths get big. No grass is on
this yak path.

Zeb can look up. Zeb can see
lots of blue. Zeb can see the sun.
Zeb is one glad yak! Zeb will go
thud, thud, thud.

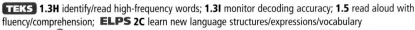
TEKS **1.3H** identify/read high-frequency words; **1.3I** monitor decoding accuracy; **1.5** read aloud with fluency/comprehension; **ELPS 2C** learn new language structures/expressions/vocabulary

Fluency

Words to Know Practice reading these words with a partner.

blue	cold	little	live

Read "Zeb Yak" with a partner. Take turns reading aloud. Read each word carefully. Check each other to see if you read these words correctly—<u>blue</u>, <u>cold</u>, <u>little</u>, <u>live</u>.

Phonics

Words with -s, -es, -ed, -ing

Read the words in the box.

Use the words to complete the sentences.

quacks   resting   jumped   fixes

1. The cat is _____.

2. That pup has _____ up.

3. The man _____ a truck.

4. This duck
   _____ a lot.

Animal Moms

by James Wang

This mom has pups. She is resting on the rocks with them. Rest, pups. Rest, mom.

This mom has cubs. The cubs
are just like their mom. They can
swim in this cold water! Swim,
cubs. Swim, mom.

This mom is hunting with her cubs.
What is jumping in that water?
Hunt, cubs! Grab a snack!

This mom is with her kits. They
swim in a pond. Their pond has
lots of sticks, grasses, and twigs.
Swim, kits. Swim, mom.

This mom is with her pups.
Their pond is filled with mud.
They can swim fast in wet mud.
Swim, pups. Swim, mom.

This mom is with her little ducks.
Ducks swim and swim. It is fun.
Have fun, ducks! Swim, swim, swim!

24

TEKS 1.14B identify important facts/details; ELPS 1C use strategic learning techniques to acquire vocabulary; 3D speak using content-area vocabulary

Facts

Information from Text What important facts did you learn about animal mothers and babies from "Animal Moms?"

Share information Pick two animals you read about. Talk with a partner about how they are the same and different.

Phonics

Words with <u>ch</u> and <u>tch</u> Add the letters and read the words. Listen for the sound like the beginning of <u>chip</u>. Then read the sentences. Point to and reread words with <u>ch</u> or <u>tch</u>.

ch + at = <u>ch</u>at

ma + tch = ma<u>tch</u>

1. Chad and Van play catch.

2. Mitch chops
   nuts for lunch.

26

Scratch, Chomp

by Edward Bonfanti

illustrated by Rick Brown

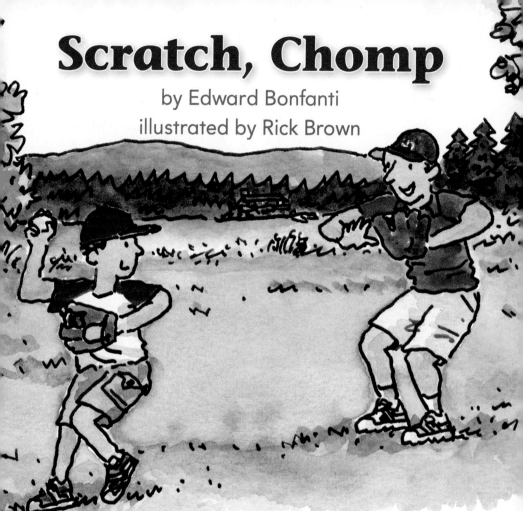

Chuck and his dad went off on a trip. At Finch Pond, Chuck and his dad played catch. Chuck has a fast pitch.

Dad can catch, but Dad did not catch this pitch.

"You never miss, Dad. Why did you miss?" Chuck asks.

"I hear scratch, scratch, chomp,
chomp. Do you?" asks Dad.
"Yes! Scratch, scratch, chomp,
chomp. What is it?" asks Chuck.

Scratch, scratch, scratch. Chomp, chomp, chomp. Can Chuck and Dad find out what is scratching and chomping?

Scratch, scratch, chomp, chomp.
Chuck and Dad can see a stump
and lots of chips. A big brown
lump is in the pond.

The bump has an animal on it.
This animal can scratch, scratch,
scratch. It can chop, chop, chop,
chop. It can chomp, chomp,
chomp. Can you tell what it is?

Decoding

Read Together

Read   Read carefully.

Can you hear <u>peck</u>, <u>peck</u>?
Does it <u>scratch</u>, <u>scratch</u>?
What animal can <u>peck</u> and
<u>scratch</u>? Is it a chick?

Think   Did you read every
word correctly? If not, look
again at the letters. Say the
sounds the letters stand for.
Now read the sentences again.
Did you read the words better?

Phonics

Words with <u>ch</u> and <u>tch</u> Read each sentence and match it to a picture. Point to and reread words with <u>ch</u> or <u>tch</u>.

1. Chuck can stitch a patch.

2. A chick will scratch and peck.

3. Mitch and Beth like to sketch.

4. Chip and Chet munch lunch on a branch.

Rich Gets a Dog

by Rick Eduardo

illustrated by Beth Spiegel

Mom and Dad tucked Rich in bed.

"Can I get a dog?" asked Rich.

"Hmmm," said Dad.

"Hmmm," said Mom.

Then Mom and Dad said yes.
Rich sat up in bed. Mom, Dad,
and Rich like dogs very much.

Today, Mom and Dad will get Rich
a dog. Rich can see dogs, dogs,
dogs. Rich can get just one dog.

Here are big dogs and small
dogs. Here are fat dogs and
thin dogs. Dogs, dogs, dogs!

Rich picks a brown dog called
Fletch. Fletch is big and can
run fast. Rich has his own dog!

Rich hugs Fletch. Fletch and Rich
will be pals.

TEKS 1.17A generate ideas for writing; 1.17B develop drafts; ELPS 5B write using new basic/ content-based vocabulary

Writing

Ideas Draw pictures of different kinds of dogs you have seen.

Write Circle the dog you like best. Write sentences that tell what this dog is like.

This dog is ____.

This dog has ____.

Phonics

Names and Words with 's

Follow the directions. Then point to and reread words with 's.

1. Find Mom's dog.

2. Find Dad's cat.

3. Where is Mitch's chick?

4. Where is Val's frog?

Kits, Chicks, and Pups

by Lara Heisman

Cats, dogs, and ducks have
moms and dads.

Dog moms have pups. This mom
and her pups sit still. They make
such a good picture.

Ducks do not have pups. Ducks
have chicks. Ducks swim in a
pond. Dad duck is with his chicks.

This mom duck has a nest. Eggs
will hatch in it. Chicks will pop
out! Mom will get off the nest.

This kit can run. Mom cat will
run, too. The kit and her mom
will run and then stop and nap.

This mom and dad know that
chicks must eat. This mom's chicks
will get fed. Mom and dad will
do it. The chicks will get big.

TEKS 1.28 share information/ideas by speaking clearly; **ELPS 3E** share information in cooperative learning interactions

Speaking

Share information Think about what you have learned about young animals. Share the information with a small group. Use these tips.

Speaking Tips

- Tell facts you have learned.
- Speak clearly and loudly enough to be heard.
- Do not speak too fast or too slowly.
- Use complete sentences.

Phonics

Words with <u>sh</u>, <u>wh</u>, <u>ph</u> Read the sentences and match them to the pictures. Then point to and reread words with <u>sh</u>, <u>wh</u>, or <u>ph</u>.

1. You can see fish and shells.

2. I make a graph in math class.

3. Whack! Phil bats the ball.

Phil's New Bat

by Edward Bonfanti

illustrated by Jennifer H. Hayden

Phil's dad got him a new bat.
It was just what Phil wished for!

When Phil got his new bat, he
hit with it. When Phil got a hit,
his bat went, "Wham! Bash!"

Phil got many hits and runs. His mom and his dad and his pal had fun! Did Phil get a hit? Yes!

Did Phil fall? Yes! Phil fell
down on his leg. Phil cannot
play with his bat for a bit.

Phil is not sad. If Phil cannot
play with his bat, Phil will let his
pal play with it.

Phil's bat is in good hands.
Phil and his dad can play catch.
You do not catch with a bat!

TEKS 1.4B ask questions/seek clarification/locate details about texts; **ELPS** 4G demonstrate comprehension through shared reading/retelling/responding/note-taking

Questions

Ask Questions Ask yourself questions like these to better understand **Phil's New Bat** on pages 51–56.

- How did Phil feel when he got his new bat?
- What happened when Phil fell down?
- Why did Phil let his pal play with his bat?

Reread the story to figure out the answers. Share your ideas with a partner.

Phonics

Words with <u>sh</u>, <u>wh</u>, <u>ph</u> Read all the words. Then find four words in a row that begin with <u>wh</u> and read them. Find four words in a row that end with <u>sh</u> and read them.

ship	graph	shop	shelf
when	which	whip	whisk
dish	crush	fish	splash
shed	wham	Phil	shell

In a Rush

by Sue De Marco
illustrated by Maria Maddocks

Shan is in a rush. She has to
splash in cold, wet slush. She
goes splish, splash, splish, splash.

59

Wham! Slip! Slop! Bash! Shan
fell down in the wet slush. Shan
just sat in slush. It felt like mush.

Then Shan got up. Shan did not
rush. Shan did not dash in the
wet slush. Shan went plop, plod.

Plop, plop, plod. Shan must get to Phil's Best Stuff Shop. That shop has lots and lots of stuff. Shan must get to that shop.

Phil's Best Stuff Shop is still open!
Shan got to it at last. Shan will
rush in. Shan has cash. What
new stuff will Shan get?

Look at Shan! Shan is all in
yellow. Slush is fun now. Shan
is glad. Splish, splash, splish,
splash, Shan!

Retelling

Discuss Plot Talk with a partner about Shan's problem and how she solves it.

Write Think about a problem you have had. Write a short story about how you solved the problem. Draw a picture to go with it.

Phonics

Contractions Read the words and contractions. Then read the sentences. Tell what two words form each contraction.

it + is = it's   is + not = isn't
he + is = he's   did + not = didn't

1. Where's Mom?
2. She's helping Phil.

3. That shell didn't crack.
4. The eggs aren't fresh.

Trish's Gift

by Bryn Haddock

illustrated by Mircea Catusanu

When Trish was ten, Gramps sent
a gift. Trish and Mom opened it.
It was a new desk.

"Dad," said Trish, "Gramps sent this desk with brass trim, but I can't sit at it,"
"Let's see that desk with brass trim," said Dad.

"Back when I was just ten," said
Dad, "I had a bench with brass
trim on it. I got big, but that
bench with brass trim didn't
grow big."
"Where is that bench?" asked Trish.

"Gramps put that bench in his shed," said Dad.

"Is that the shed Gramps had?" asked Trish.

"Yes, it's his shed," said Dad.

Dad and Trish ran fast.

Trish and Dad hunted and hunted.
Then Dad lifted up a big green
cloth.
"That's it!" yelled Trish.

"Did Gramps know that we
had this bench with brass trim?"
asked Trish.
"We can ask him," said Dad.
"Let's call Gramps and ask."

Fluency

End Marks Read these sentences from "Trish's Gift." Each sentence should sound different. Use the end marks to help you.

> **It was a new desk.**
> **Where is that bench?**
> **That's it!**

Read Aloud Work with a partner. Use end marks to help you read aloud the story.

73

Phonics

Words with Long <u>a</u> Read the words. Listen for the short <u>a</u> and the long <u>a</u> sounds. Then read the sentences. Point to and reread the long <u>a</u> words.

can + e = cane   mad + e = made

tap + e = tape   pal + e = pale

1. Let's bake a cake.

2. Jane ate some grapes.

3. Dave can wade in the lake.

Tate's Cakes

by Bruce Falcon
illustrated by Peter Grosshauser

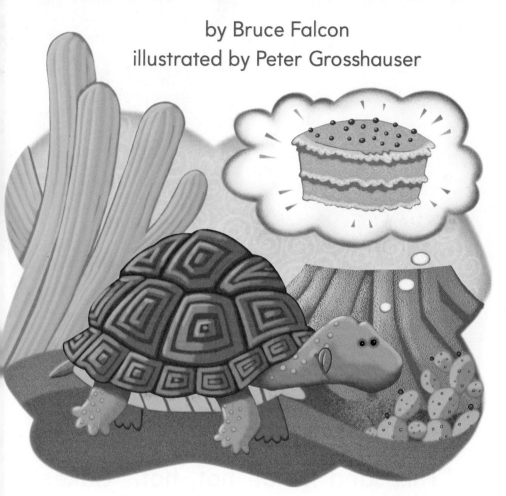

Tate had never made a cake.
Tate did know that cakes must
bake. Can Tate make cakes?

"This sand is hot, hot, hot. Cakes can bake in it. What goes into cakes? If Wade has made cakes, Wade will tell me," said Tate.

"Well, I never made a cake,"
said Wade. "Let's ask Jade. If
Jade has made cakes, Jade will
tell us."
"Yes," said Tate, "let's ask Jade."

Wade and Tate went to Jade's big cave. Jade was in.

"I am glad you came," said Jade.

"I just made ten cakes."

"This cake is on sale. That cake is
on sale and that cake is on sale.
The big cakes are all on sale,"
Jade said. "I just made them."

Wade got four cakes. Tate got
five cakes. Jade's bake sale was
over. Tate and Wade ate Jade's
cakes. Tate and Wade never did
make cakes. They ate Jade's.

TEKS 1.17A generate ideas for writing; **1.19A** write brief compositions; **1.20A(iii)** understand/use adjectives; **ELPS 5B** write using new basic/content-based vocabulary

Writing

Read Together

Plan to Write Look at Jade's cakes. Which one would you like to get? Draw a picture of it.

Describe Write sentences to tell your classmates about the cake. Use adjectives to tell how it looks, smells, and tastes.

Phonics

Words with Long <u>a</u> Read the words. Use one of the words in a sentence. Then use two of the words in a sentence.

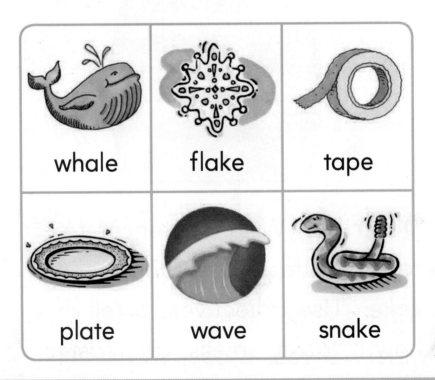

whale

flake

tape

plate

wave

snake

Dave and the Whales

by Andrew Hathaway
illustrated by Julia Woolf

Dave is a whale. Dave is fast.
"Let's play," Dave yelled. "Chase
me! Chase, chase, chase me!"

Dave's pals watch. Not one whale
is as fast as Dave is. Dave did
not get his pals to chase him.
"Why chase Dave?" asked Jake.
"We can't catch him."

Dave made waves as big as hills.
"Let's make waves!" yelled Dave.
"Why?" asked Lane. "We can't
make waves as big as Dave's."
Dave did not get his pals to make
waves.

Dave is sad. His pals will not play with him.

"I get it," said Dave. "I am fast and can make big waves. But, I can't sing!"

"Let's sing!" yelled Dave.
Two whales came. Three whales
came. Then four and five whales
came.

"Sing, whales!" yelled Dave. "Let's
make a tape. Let's name it Dave
and the Whales! It will be a big
hit!"

TEKS **1.1A** recognize that print represents speech; **RC-1(E)** retell/act out important story events; **ELPS 1E** internalize new basic/academic language

Words in Print

Read Together

Dialogue Print can show words people say. With two partners, read these sentences.

> **Dave:** "Let's go fast and make waves!"
>
> **Jake:** "I can't go fast, but I can sing."
>
> **Lane:** "I can't make waves, but I can sing."
>
> **Dave:** "Then let's all sing."

Act out what Dave, Jake, and Lane say with your partners.

Phonics

Words with Soft <u>c</u> and Soft <u>g</u>

Read each word pair. Say the sound for the underlined letter or letters. Is the sound the same or different in the two words?

<u>c</u>ent	pla<u>ce</u>	<u>g</u>em	bad<u>ge</u>
<u>s</u>and	ga<u>s</u>	<u>j</u>ump	pa<u>g</u>e

Read the sentence. Reread the words with underlined letters. Which stand for the same sound?

Ma<u>dg</u>e and <u>J</u>ane ra<u>c</u>e to the bu<u>s</u>.

The Race

by Carre Murray
illustrated by Jerry Smath

This race is fun to watch. Get
into the fun! Yell, yell. Clap,
clap. Race, race, race!

Dave and Ace got in this race.
Dave will run fast. Ace will run
fast. Crack! The race starts.
Dave and Ace take off.

Dave has a lane. It is his space.
Ace has a lane. It is his space.
They must run and jump in that
lane. They can't trade lanes.

Madge and Grace got in this
race. They will skate fast. Go,
Madge! Go, Grace! Skate as
fast as you can. Race, race, race.

Blake and Trace got in this race.
Blake and Trace set the pace.
Will Trace race past Blake? Go,
Blake! Go, Trace!

The last race is over. Madge,
Grace, Blake, Trace, Dave, and
Ace sit in the shade. The judge
gave two of them red badges
and four of them blue badges.

TEKS 1.3A(ii) decode words with vowels; 1.3D decode words with common spelling patterns; 1.6D categorize words; ELPS 4A learn English sound-letter relationships/decode

Spelling Patterns

Sort Words   Read the words:

| race   Trace   late   stage   skate |

Copy this chart.

_ace	_age	_ate

Write each word from the green box in the correct column. How are the words in each column alike? Add more words and read them.

TEKS **1.3A(i)** decode words in isolation; **1.3C(iv)** decode using VCe pattern; **1.3D** decode words with common spelling patterns

Phonics

Words with Long i Read all the words. Find three words with long i in a row. Reread those words. Then find and reread three words that do not have the long i sound. Tell what vowel sound those words have.

bike	strips	five
white	stripe	prize
ditch	rice	six

Mike's Bike

by Claire Coolidge
illustrated by Jill Dubin

Mike's new bike is red and white.
Mike just got it. Mike can ride
it well. Mike rides his bike
with pride.

Mike will ride his bike to see Nell.
His dad will ride with him. Nell
will like Mike's bike. Nell's bike is
red and white, too.

Nell did like Mike's bike.
"I like its white stripes. Mine
has red stripes. Both bikes have
stripes," Nell said.

Mike, Dad, and Nell take a ride.
"This bike path is fun. I like it,"
said Mike. "It is nice to ride on."
"I like it too," said Nell.

Dad, Nell, and Mike ride for five
or six miles. It is a long ride.
"This is the end," said Nell. "It is
time to go back."

They stop at Nell's place.

"That was fun, Mike," said Nell.

Mike had a big, wide grin on
his face.

"Best time of my life!" said Mike.

TEKS **1.6A** identify nouns/verbs; **1.6D** categorize words; **ELPS 1C** use strategic learning techniques to acquire vocabulary

Vocabulary

Verbs and Nouns Words that name actions are verbs. Nouns name people or things. Read these words.

> bike   ride   Mike   go   Dad

Copy this chart.

Actions	People	Things

Write the words from the green box in the correct columns. Add more.

TEKS 1.3A(i) decode words in context and in isolation; **1.3C(iv)** decode using VCe pattern; **1.3D** decode words with common spelling patterns

Phonics

Words with Long <u>i</u> Read the questions. Point to and reread words with the long <u>i</u> sound. Then answer the questions. Use the pictures to help you.

1. What is black and white?

2. What can tell time?

3. What do mice like?

The Nest

by Amy Long

This big bird has a name. His name is Pale Male. Pale Male's chest is white. Pale Male's neck is white.

Pale Male has a nest. The nest
is wide. It is a big, big nest. Pale
Male made it. It can take a long
time to make a big nest like this.

If you walk past it, look up. Pale Male's nest is not just a big pile of sticks and vines. It is a fine nest.

The nest had eggs in it. It has
small chicks in it now. Dad and
Mom find mice for them. Those
chicks get quite big, as big as
Mom and Dad.

It is time to fly. Chicks grasp the
nest at its side. Chicks flap and
flap and flap. Then they let go
and glide. Glide, flap, flap, glide.
Both can fly!

This big chick can fly like Mom and Dad. This chick can rise up and dip down. Rise and dive, chick. Rise and glide, chick. Fly!

TEKS 1.14C retell order of events; ELPS 4G demonstrate comprehension through shared reading/retelling/responding/note-taking

Retelling

Order of Events Think about the story "The Nest." These story events are all mixed up.

- Chicks fly.
- There are eggs in the nest.
- Pale Male makes a nest.
- Dad and mom find mice for chicks.

Work with a partner. Retell the events in the correct order by using the words in the story.

Phonics

Words with <u>kn</u>, <u>wr</u>, <u>gn</u>, <u>mb</u>

Read the words. Use the words to complete the sentences.

write   knife   lamb   gnats

1. Cut the cake with this _____.

2. Some _____ can bite you.

3. I will _____ my name.

4. Mike has a pet duck and a pet _____.

Kite Time

by Zach Mathews
illustrated by Chi Chung

The wind is up. It's time to fly a
kite. It's kite time! It's fun time!

A kite can ride on the wind. It can glide up on the wind. Wind takes a kite up and up. Wind can knock it down, too.

A kite can dip down. Then it can
rise back up. A kite can dip or
rise. It can rise, dip, and rise.
Wind can play with it.

Make fists and run with the kite's
line in them. Run with it. Run,
run, run. Run fast! Then the kite
will fly like a bird. Up, up, up it
will rise.

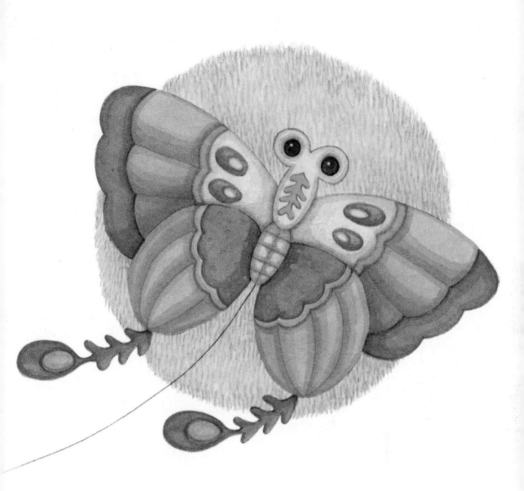

It is up. Then it dips. It is up.
Then it glides. It is up. Then it
dives. It is up. Then it slides.
Hold on to the kite's line. Do not
let it go!

If the wind stops, it's time to quit.
Wrap up the kites.

TEKS **1.14B** Identify important facts/details; **1.14D** use text features to locate information; **1.24C** record information in visual formats

Details

Important Details With a partner, read "Kite Time" again. Look at the pictures. Identify important details in the text about how to fly a kite.

Together, make a list of important details about how to fly a kite.

How to Fly a Kite

1.
2.
3.
4.

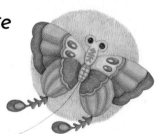

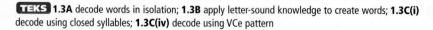
TEKS **1.3A** decode words in isolation; **1.3B** apply letter-sound knowledge to create words; **1.3C(i)** decode using closed syllables; **1.3C(iv)** decode using VCe pattern

Phonics

Read to Review   Use what you know about sounds and letters to read the words.

Words with kn, wr, gn, mb

knot	knit	knock	knife
write	wrap	gnat	lamb

Words with sh, wh, ph

ship	shell	fish	wishes
when	whale	which	whisk
Phil	graph	Ralph	graphs

Words with dge

edge	badge	fudge	judge
ledge	lodge	bridge	pledge

Words with <u>kn</u>, <u>wr</u>, <u>mb</u>

knob	knack	knots	knocking
wrist	wreck	wrench	numb

Words with <u>sh</u>, <u>wh</u>, <u>ph</u>

shade	shine	dishes	splash
when	whales	graph	Ralph

Build and Read Words   Put the letters together to read the words.
Think of more words to add.

b	ake		f	udge
c	ake		j	udge
sh	ake		s m	udge

TEKS 1.3A(i) decode words with consonants; **1.3A(ii)** decode words with vowels; **1.3A(iv)** decode words with consonant digraphs

Phonics

Words with <u>tch</u> Read each word by itself. Find three words with <u>tch</u> in a row. Reread those words. Tell what vowel sound each word has.

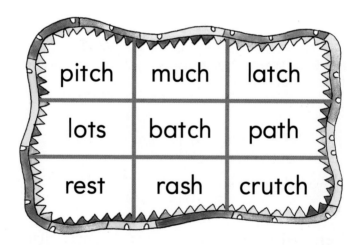

pitch	much	latch
lots	batch	path
rest	rash	crutch

Phonics

Decode Words in Isolation   Put the letters together to read each
word by itself. Think of more words to add.

b atch	**d** ish
c atch	**f** ish
p atch	**w** ish
d ine	**f** ace
l ine	**p** ace
p ine	**r** ace

Word Lists

Seth and Beth

page 2

Decodable Words
Target Skill: Digraph *th*
Beth, path, Seth, them, then, this, with

Previously Taught Skills
and, asks, at, Ben, big, Bob, can, cap, Duck, Frog, fun, get, has, hats, help, his, Huck, in, is, it, map, met, pass, pond, Sam, tip, tips, trip, up, us, will, yells

High-Frequency Words
New
blue, far, live, their, where

Previously Taught
a, are, call, does, go, here, play, see, the, they

Zeb Yak

page 10

Decodable Words
Target Skill: Digraph *th*
path, paths, then, this, thud, thump, with

Previously Taught Skills
and, big, can, cut, dad, get, glad, grass, hill, his, is, lots, mom, nap, not, on, sun, up, will, yak, yaks, yet, Zeb

High-Frequency Words
New
blue, cold, little, live

Previously Taught
a, be, eat, go, like, look, no, of, one, see, the

Animal Moms

page 18

Decodable Words
Target Skill: Endings *-s, -es, -ed, -ing*
cubs, ducks, filled, grasses, hunting, jumping, kits, lots, moms, pups, resting, rocks, sticks, twigs

Target Skill: Digraph *th*
that, them, this, with

Previously Taught Skills
and, can, fast, fun, grab, has, hunt, in, is, it, just, mom, mud, on, pond, rest, snack, swim, wet

High-Frequency Words
New
cold, little, their, water

Previously Taught
a, animal, are, have, her, like, of, she, the, they, what

127

Scratch, Chomp

page 26

Decodable Words
Target Skill: Digraphs *ch*, *tch*
catch, chips, chomp, chomping, chop, Chuck, Finch, pitch, scratch, scratching

Previously Taught Skills
an, and, asks, at, big, but, can, dad, did, fast, has, his, in, is, it, lots, lump, miss, not, off, on, pond, stump, tell, this, trip, went, yes

High-Frequency Words
New
brown, never, off, out

Previously Taught
a, animal, do, find, hear, I, of, played, see, the, what, why, you

Rich Gets a Dog

page 34

Decodable Words
Target Skill: Digraphs *ch*, *tch*
Fletch, much, Rich

Previously Taught Skills
and, asked, bed, big, can, Dad, dog, dogs, fast, fat, get, gets, has, his, Hmmm, hugs, in, just, Mom, pals, picks run, sat, then, thin, tucked, up, will, yes

High-Frequency Words
New
brown, own, very

Previously Taught
a, are, be, called, here, I, like, one, said, see, small, today

128

Kits, Chicks, and Pups

page 42

Decodable Words
Target Skill: Possessives with 's
mom's

Target Skill: Digraphs *ch*, *tch*
chicks, hatch, such

Previously Taught Skills
and, big, can, cat, cats, dad, dads, dog,
dogs, duck, ducks, eggs, fed, get, has,
his, in, is, it, kits, moms, must, nap,
nest, not, off, pond, pop, pups, run,
stop, swim, that, this, then, will, with

High-Frequency Words
New
know, off, out

Previously Taught
a, do, eat, good, have, her,
in, picture, the, too

129

Accompanies *"Seasons"*

Phil's New Bat

page 50

Decodable Words
Target Skill: Digraphs *sh, wh, ph*
bash, Phil, Phil's, wham, when, wished

Previously Taught Skills
and, bat, bit, can, cannot, catch, dad, did,
fell, fun, get, got, hands, him, his, hit,
hits, if, in, is, it, just, leg, let, mom, not,
on, pal, runs, sad, went, will, with, yes

High-Frequency Words
New
down, fall, new

Previously Taught
a, do, for, good, he, many,
play, was, what, you

In a Rush

page 58

Decodable Words
Target Skill: Digraphs *sh, wh, ph*
bash, cash, dash, mush, Phil's, rush,
Shan, shop, slush, splash, splish, wham

Previously Taught Skills
and, at, best, did, fell, felt, fun, get, glad,
got, has, in, is, it, just, last, lots, must,
not, plod, plop, sat, slip, slop, still, stuff,
that, then, up, went, wet, will

High-Frequency Words
New
down, goes, open, yellow

Previously Taught
a, all, cold, like, look, now,
of, she, the, to, what

Trish's Gift

page 66

Decodable Words
Target Skill: Contractions *'s*, *n't*
can't, didn't, it's, let's, that's

Target Skill: Digraphs *sh*, *wh*, *ph*
shed, Trish, Trish's, when

Previously Taught Skills
and, ask, asked, at, back, bench, big,
brass, but, cloth, Dad, did, desk, fast,
gift, got, Gramps, had, him, his, hunted,
in, is, it, just, lifted, on, ran, sent, sit, ten,
that, then, this, trim, up, with, yelled,
yes

High-Frequency Words
New
green, grow, new, open

Previously Taught
a, call, I, know, put, said,
see, the, was, we, where

Tate's Cakes
page 74

Decodable Words
Target Skill: Long *a* (CVC*e*)
ate, bake, cake, cakes, came, cave, Jade,
Jade's, made, make, sale, Tate, Wade

Previously Taught Skills
am, and, ask, big, can, did, glad, got,
had, has, hot, if, in, is, it, just, let's, must,
on, sand, tell, ten, that, them, this, us,
well, went, will, yes

High-Frequency Words
New
four, five, into, over

Previously Taught
a, are, goes, I, know, me,
never, said, the, they, to,
was, what, you

Dave and the Whales
page 82

Decodable Words
Target Skill: Long *a* (CVC*e*)
came, chase, Dave, Dave's, Jake, Lane,
made, make, name, tape, waves, whale,
whales

Previously Taught Skills
am, and, as, asked, big, but, can, can't,
catch, did, fast, get, hills, him, his, hit,
is, it, let's, not, pals, sad, then, will, with,
yelled

High-Frequency Words
New
five, four, three, two, watch

Previously Taught
a, be, I, me, one, play, said,
sing, the, to, we, why

The Race

page 90

Decodable Words
Target Skills: Soft *c*, *g*, *dge*
Ace, badges, Grace, judge, Madge, pace, race, space, Trace

Target Skill: Long *a* (CVC*e*)
Ace, Blake, Dave, gave, Grace, lane, lanes, pace, race, shade, skate, space, take, Trace, trade

Previously Taught Skills
and, as, can, can't, clap, crack, fast, fun, get, got, has, his, in, is, it, jump, last, must, off, past, red, run, set, sit, that, them, this, will, yell

High-Frequency Words
New
four, into, over, starts, two, watch

Previously Taught
a, blue, go, of, the, they, to, you

133

Mike's Bike

page 98

Decodable Words
Target Skill: Long *i* (CVC*e*)
bike, bikes, five, life, like, Mike, Mike's, miles, mine, nice, pride, ride, rides, stripes, time, white, wide

Previously Taught Skills
and, at, back, best, big, can, dad, did, end, face, fun, got, grin, had, has, him, his, is, it, its, just, Nell, Nell's, on, path, place, red, six, stop, take, that, this, well, will, with

High-Frequency Words
New
both, long, or

Previously Taught
a, for, go, have, I, my, new, of, said, see, the, they, to, too, was

The Nest

page 106

Decodable Words
Target Skill: Long *i* (CVC*e*)
fine, glide, like, mice, pile, quite, rise, side, time, vines, white, wide

Previously Taught Skills
and, as, at, big, can, chest, chick, chicks, Dad, dip, eggs, flap, get, grasp, had, has, if, in, is, it, its, just, let, make, made, Male, Male's, Mom, name, neck, nest, not, Pale, past, sticks, take, them, then, this, up

High-Frequency Words
New
bird, both, fly, long, those, walk

Previously Taught
a, down, find, for, go, look, now, of, small, the, they, to, you

Kite Time

page 114

Decodable Words
Target Skill: Digraphs *kn*, *wr*
wrap, knock

Target Skill: Long *i* (CVC*e*)
dives, glide, glides, kite, kite's, like, line, ride, rise, slides, time

Previously Taught Skills
and, back, can, dip, dips, fast, fist, fun, if, in, is, it, it's, let, make, not, on, quit, run, stops, takes, them, then, up, will, wind, with

High-Frequency Words
New
bird, fly, or

Previously Taught
a, do, down, go, hold, play, the, to, too